This Book Belongs To:

....

....

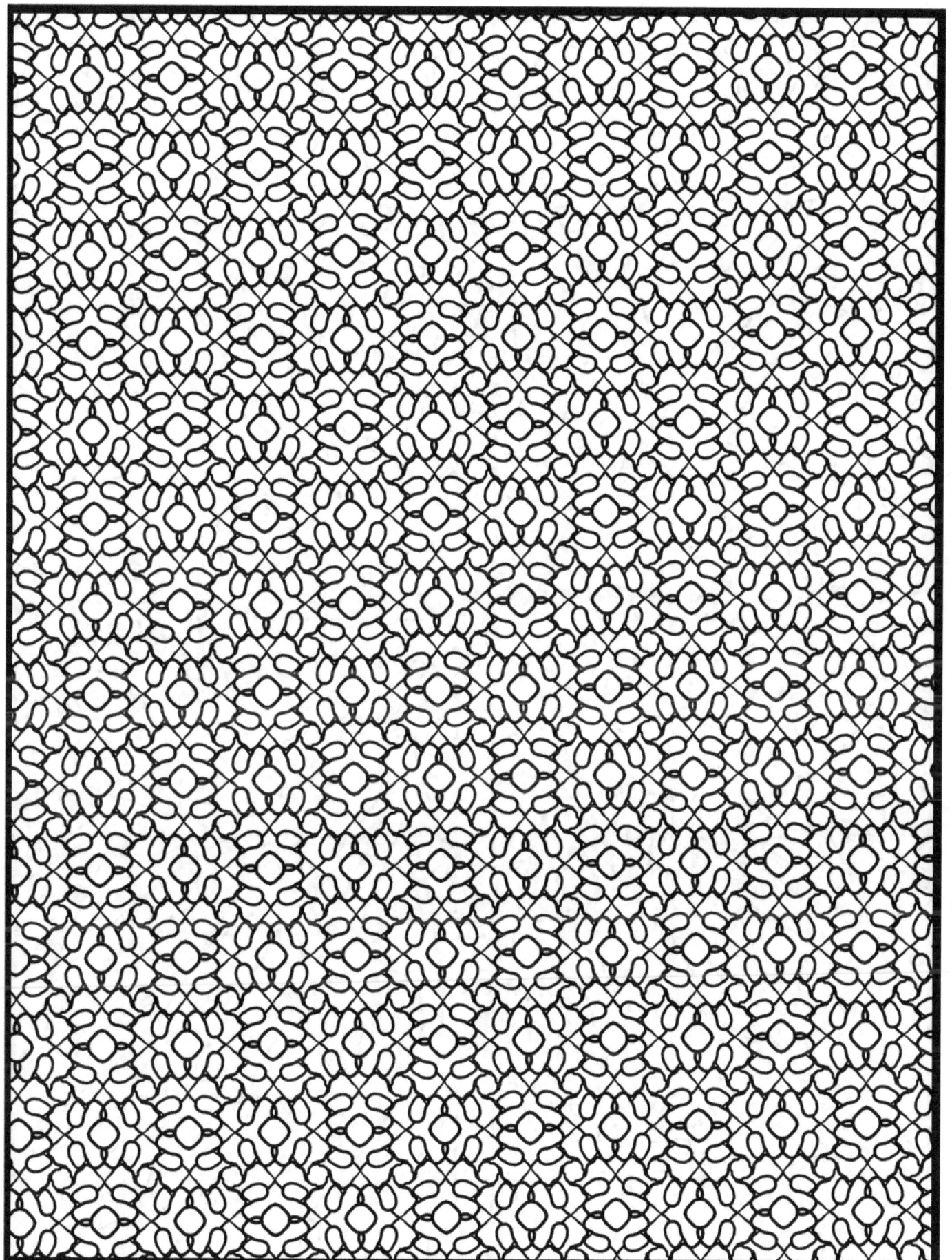

www.ingramcontent.com/pod-product-compliance
Lightning Source LLC
Chambersburg PA
CBHW081445220526
45466CB00008B/2517